CONTEN

MW01055369

INTRODUCTION

Decoupage (from the French, *découpe*, to cut out) entails gluing cutout pictures to an object and covering with varnish. It's a fun and easy way to decorate just about anything, from small pieces of jewelry to large items of furniture. Discover how simple it is to personalize your favourite things with these seventeen gorgeous projects. With plenty of ideas for fabulous decorative effects, we're sure you'll enjoy making them.

TIN CANS

Turn tin cans into handy storage containers with this quick upcycle, and organize everything from craft supplies to kitchen utensils.

MATERIALS
- Tins, cleaned thoroughly and dried (choose ones that don't need to be opened with a can opener so the edges are smooth)
- Decorative fabric or paper
- Tape measure and scissors
- PVA (white) glue, diluted 50:50 with water
- Small paintbrush
- Slightly damp sponge
- Plastic sheet or newspaper

1 Lay out the plastic sheet or newspaper to protect your work surface. Measure the tin, then cut out a piece of fabric ¾in (2cm) higher than the tin and ¾in (2cm) longer than its circumference.

2 Fold the two long edges and one short edge over by ⅜in (1cm). Stick down with glue.

3 Using a paintbrush, coat half the tin with a thin layer of watered-down glue. Wrap the fabric tightly around the glued half

then glue the rest of the tin and wrap the rest of the fabric around it. Stick down the overlap with glue and wipe off any excess with the sponge. Leave to dry for at least 30 minutes.

4 For a hardwearing finish, paint more coats of glue on top of the fabric. The glue will appear white at first but will dry clear. Let each coat dry completely before applying the next. Wash out the paintbrush between applications so you can reuse it.

CLIPBOARD

Decoupage is a great way to pretty up plain items of stationery and make them stand out in a crowd.

MATERIALS

- Clipboard
- A3 sheet of plain paper
- Ruler, pencil and scissors
- Decorative fabric or paper
- PVA (white) glue, diluted 50:50 with water
- Small paintbrush
- Slightly damp sponge
- Plastic sheet or newspaper

1 Make a pattern for the clipboard front by drawing up a template (this should be roughly ⅜in/1cm larger all around than the overall dimensions of the board) on the plain paper. Take time to work out the shape around the metal clip.

2 Cut another template the same size as the clipboard, then cut it slightly smaller all the way around. This is for the back and should be glued on last. Use the templates to cut out the fabric.

3 Protect the work surface with the plastic sheet. Paint a thin layer of glue on the front of the clipboard, not on the fabric.

4 Smooth out the fabric and keep a clean, slightly damp sponge handy to wipe away any smudges of glue as quickly as possible. Glue the edge of the board and ⅜in (1cm) around the back before folding the fabric over, smoothing it down as you go.

5 Apply glue to the back (to within a couple of mm from the edge) and stick down the backing paper or fabric. Leave to dry completely.

6 For a hardwearing finish, paint more coats of glue on top of the fabric.

FILING CABINET

Personalize office equipment by using decoupage. Here a dull filing cabinet has been transformed into something chic as well as useful.

MATERIALS

- Filing cabinet
- Decorative fabric or paper
- A3 sheet of plain paper
- Ruler, pencil and scissors
- PVA (white) glue, diluted 50:50 with water
- Small paintbrush
- Dry, soft cloth
- Slightly damp sponge
- Clear varnish
- Dust sheet or newspaper

1 Place the dust sheet or newspaper under the filing cabinet. Remove all knobs and handles. Using the sheet of A3 paper, make a template based on the size of the front of the drawers, allowing an extra ¾in (2cm) all round.

2 Using a selection of fabrics or patterned paper, cut out pieces for decoupage, marking any points that may need cutting to allow for drawer handles.

3 Apply the diluted glue to the surface of the drawers rather than the fabric or paper itself.

4 Place the fabric or paper onto the front of each drawer and smooth out using a dry, soft cloth. Wipe off any excess glue with a slightly damp sponge.

5 Fold excess fabric or paper over each edge for a clean look. For a hardwearing, waterproof finish, paint a few layers of varnish over the top. Leave to dry then reattach the drawer handles.

TIP
If you find a bubble in the paper after it has dried, pop it with a pin then cover with a small amount of diluted PVA glue and press down.

TILES

Give your kitchen a whole new look with decoupaged tiles, or make a set of stylish coasters.

MATERIALS

- Plain glazed tiles
- Decoupage paper, or scraps of wrapping paper or wallpaper
- Felt (if making coasters)
- Ruler, pencil and scissors
- PVA (white) glue, diluted 50:50 with water
- Small paintbrush
- Slightly damp sponge
- Clear varnish
- Plastic sheet or newspaper

1 Measure the area for the paper cutouts to sit on the tiles, leaving a small border on all sides. Cut out pieces of paper to the required size. If making coasters, cut out squares of felt backing to a size slightly smaller than the tiles.

2 Lay out the plastic sheet to protect your work surface. Paint a thin layer of diluted PVA glue onto the tiles and on the back of each paper cutout. Leave for five minutes to ensure the paper doesn't bubble when stuck down.

3 Place cutouts on the tiles and smooth out any bubbles with the paintbrush or your fingers. Wipe off excess glue with the sponge and leave to dry.

4 For coasters: apply glue to the back of the tiles and place a felt square on top. Leave to dry.

5 Apply a coat of varnish to the front of each tile, making sure you cover the whole of the image. Wipe off any excess around the border. Leave to dry for at least two hours and apply another coat or more if required.

WINE BOX

Transform an old wine box into a stylish container
with a little help from some decoupage.

MATERIALS

- Wooden wine box
- Decorative paper
- Scissors or craft knife (optional)
- PVA (white) glue, diluted 50:50 with water
- Small paintbrush
- Slightly damp sponge
- Bowl of water
- Clear varnish (optional)
- Plastic sheet or newspaper

1 Lay out the plastic sheet or newspaper on your work surface. Make sure the box is clean and dry. Either tear up or cut the decorative paper into small pieces roughly 4in (10cm) across.

2 Using the paintbrush, apply a thin layer of glue to one side of the box. Place the pieces of paper on top, smooth out any wrinkles and wipe off excess glue with the sponge. Rinse out the sponge as required. Keep going until the outside and inside of the box is covered.

3 Leave the box to dry completely, and smooth over any air bubbles or raised edges that you notice.

4 Paint with another coat of PVA to seal the paper or use clear varnish instead.

TIP
Wash out your paintbush before the glue has dried so you can use it again.

WOODEN CHAIR

Selecting the paper is always the fun part of decoupage. Here we have used maps to cover an old chair, but you can experiment with anything from seed packets to sheet music for your own one-off creation.

MATERIALS
- Wooden chair
- Decorative paper
- Scissors or craft knife (optional)
- Sandpaper
- PVA (white) glue, diluted 50:50 with water
- Small paintbrush
- Small roller
- Slightly damp sponge
- Clear varnish
- Dust sheet or newspaper

1 Lay out the dust sheet or newspaper underneath the chair. Clean and sand the chair until it is smooth. Tear up or cut the paper into small pieces roughly 4in (10cm) across.

2 Paint a thin layer of watered-down glue onto the back of the paper and then stick it onto the chair. Wipe off excess glue and smooth out the wrinkles using the sponge and the roller as you go. Repeat with each piece of paper and keep going until you've covered everything. You will find it easier to use small pieces for corners and curves.

3 Smooth over any air bubbles or raised edges and leave to dry completely.

4 For a hard-wearing, waterproof finish, paint the chair with at least four coats of varnish, leaving each coat to dry completely before applying the next. The more coats of varnish you use, the smoother the finish will be.

5 Leave the chair to dry completely before using – this will take at least 24 hours.

TIP
If you paint your chair with a latex primer before you start the decoupage (leave the paint to dry thoroughly first), the paper will stick better.

CHEST OF DRAWERS

Give an old chest of drawers a fresh new look with some clever decoupage. With a careful choice of papers and some modern colours, you'll end up with a piece that looks hand painted and contemporary.

MATERIALS
- Furniture and decorative paper
- Medium-grade sandpaper
- Acrylic primer and eggshell paint
- 1½in (4cm) paintbrush
- Artist's paintbrush and paint
- Cutting mat and scalpel
- PVA (white) glue, diluted 50:50 with water
- Slightly damp sponge
- Water-based matte varnish
- Dust sheet or newspaper

1 Find an old chest of drawers, or other piece of furniture of your choice. Lay out the dust sheet and, with a medium grade sandpaper, rub back the surface gently to remove varnish or to key the existing finish.

2 After removing any handles or hardware, apply one coat of acrylic primer/ undercoat before applying two coats of acrylic eggshell paint.

TIP
For the best results, use good-quality wrapping paper.

3 Look at the papers and decide how you would like your pattern to look and which areas to cut out.

4 If you are using more than one paper, consider painting onto the design with colours to tie in the palette.

5 Cut out carefully with a sharp scalpel. When this is done, place the cutouts on a separate sheet of paper and move them around until you decide on the finished design. Take a photo for reference when you start sticking the cutouts in place.

6 Using diluted PVA glue, thoroughly coat the back of the cutouts, making sure you don't miss any bits. Let the pieces sit for five minutes to ensure the paper doesn't bubble when stuck on. Press the cutout paper onto the furniture and smooth over with a slightly damp sponge to remove wrinkles and any excess glue.

7 Leave to dry for two to three hours before applying the first coat of varnish. Following the instructions on the varnish, repeat as many coats as necessary. Four extra coats of varnish were used here to flatten out the edges of the decoupage.

TIPS
Decide before painting if you need to change the handles and fill any drill holes that aren't needed.

Mix and match wrapping paper with similar colours.

ANTIQUED SHELVES

Use cutouts from high-quality wrapping paper to create an antique effect on a wall-mounted shelving unit.

MATERIALS

- Shelving unit
- Decorative paper
- Sandpaper
- 2 pots of emulsion paint in contrasting colours
- Paintbrushes, small and medium
- Wax stick or candle
- Wire wool and craft blade
- PVA (white) glue, diluted 50:50 with water
- Slightly damp sponge
- Varnish
- Dust sheet or newspaper

1 Place the dust sheet under the shelving unit. Remove all knobs and handles. Sand the unit and dust off.

2 Paint the first coat of emulsion. Leave to dry for approximately two hours.

3 Wax liberally all over with the wax stick or candle. The wax will assist you in rubbing back to the first coat after the second coat of paint is applied.

4 Apply the top coat in the other colour of emulsion paint (and a further coat if needed). Leave to dry.

5 Create the antique effect by using sandpaper or wire wool or a craft blade. Each makes a subtle difference to the finish. Concentrate on sanding areas that would naturally wear first, as in edges and around knobs etc.

6 Now it's time to start the decoupage. A high-quality wrapping paper was used here but you can use wallpaper, magazine and book cutouts or old photographs, for example. The closer the colour of the picture to the colour of your paint, the more subtle and integrated the images will be. However, a stark contrast in colour can work, too.

7 Stick on the cutouts using diluted PVA glue. Paste the back of the images and let them sit for five minutes to ensure the paper doesn't bubble when stuck on. The aim here is to get a balanced piece. What can work to great effect is to have one image overlap two or more surfaces, say from a door to a drawer. Smooth down and wipe off any excess glue with a slightly damp sponge. Leave to dry for about one hour.

8 Now apply the top coats of varnish. Traditionally up to 40 coats of varnish were used but this is purely for visual effect, making the images look as if they had been painted or like wood inlays. Three coats should be plenty in this instance.

DESK AND CHAIR

Revamp an old school desk and chair with some crafty decoupage, and keep the subject scholarly by using old maps.

MATERIALS

- Desk and chair
- Decorative paper
- Emulsion paint and paintbrush
- 60–120 grit sandpaper
- PVA (white) glue, diluted 50:50 with water
- Small paintbrush and damp sponge
- Varnish
- Dust sheet or newspaper

1 Place the dust sheet under the desk and chair. Prepare the furniture for painting by sanding to provide a key. Make sure it is clean and completely dry before painting.

2 Apply a coat of paint and leave to dry for two hours, then sand the paint back slightly to give it an older, worn look.

3 Place the paper in position to measure it and cut to fit.

4 With the small paintbrush, apply a thin layer of glue to the desk and chair where the paper will sit and leave to dry.

5 Glue the back of the paper and leave to sit for a few minutes to minimize bubbling. Stick down the paper, smoothing as you go with a slightly damp sponge to make sure there are no bubbles and to remove excess glue.

6 The paper will almost certainly have stretched, so cut off any excess. Leave to dry for approximately five hours.

7 Apply varnish to the whole unit, then several more coats to the papered area (letting each coat dry first). Leave to dry for at least 24 hours before using.

JEWELRY STORE

Use special decoupage papers to make a beautiful set of drawers for your treasures.

MATERIALS

- MDF set of drawers, or similar
- Decoupage papers, or other decorative paper
- Scissors (optional)
- Dust sheet or newspaper
- PVA (white) glue, diluted 50:50 with water
- Small paintbrush
- Varnish

This project uses specialized decoupage papers to cover a small MDF set of drawers that were made for the purpose. This particular set of drawers has slightly loose drawers to allow for the extra depth added from the paper coat.

1 Choose your papers. Special decoupage papers, which are about A3 in size, were used in this project – two sheets each of two colours. Cut the paper or tear it into a variety of small sizes, with the biggest being about 1in (2.5cm) long.

2 Lay out the dust sheet or newspaper on your work surface. Using the paintbrush, paint a thin layer of diluted PVA glue the size of the piece of paper you want to

attach onto the piece you are covering. With the same brush, pick up a piece of paper by pressing the bristles gently on the front of the paper. Place the paper onto the glued area, then pick up a little more glue on the brush and paint over the whole piece of paper again, from the centre to the edges.

3 Glue the area next to the piece you have just done and add the next piece of paper, letting the papers overlap a little. Don't worry about lining them up perfectly as the charm of decoupage is the random placement of the paper.

4 Let all the sections dry separately then finish with a layer of varnish. Be warned: the glue takes much longer to dry than you think. It will feel touch dry very quickly, but if you then place the drawers back in the frame, they will stick and the piece will be ruined. So it's best to leave the pieces overnight to make sure they are completely dry before reassembling the drawers.

PASTING AROUND CORNERS

To patch around a corner, paint a thin layer of glue on one side then position the paper. Let the paper hang over the edge, then paint the glue on the next side and paste the paper to that side. The final side will have the paper folded, so paste down one piece then lay the final flap over the previously pasted section.

INSIDE THE DRAWERS

To stick paper inside the drawers, paint the glue on the side and base, again just working with the space that is the right size for the paper. Pick up the paper with your brush and position where the side and base meet, pushing the paper right into the corner. You can then paste it flat, working away from the centre.

INSIDE THE DRAWER FRAME

This admittedly is tricky as you need to start at the back and it's a bit fiddly and time-consuming. Use smaller pieces of paper and work in small sections to make sure you cover the whole area.

WRITING BUREAU

Show off scraps of beautiful wallpaper by decoupaging a traditional writing bureau for a fresh, contemporary look.

MATERIALS

- A piece of furniture
- Wallpaper scraps
- Sandpaper, scissors and craft knife
- Gloss spray paint
- Wallpaper paste
- PVA (white) glue, diluted 50:50 with water
- Paintbrushes in varying sizes
- Small roller (optional)
- Slighly damp sponge
- Gloss varnish
- Dust sheet or newspaper

1 Prepare the piece of furniture by lightly sanding off any old paint or varnish to create an even surface ready for painting and decoupage.

2 Next, measure the length of the surface you wish to decoupage and divide that by how many different pieces of wallpaper you would like to use. To make sure curved edges (and areas such as the compartmented shelf on the top section of this piece) are measured perfectly, lay the wallpaper down and score along the edges with your thumb then carefully cut along the score line. The wallpaper will then fit any awkwardly shaped piece perfectly.

3 Lay out all the wallpaper on the piece of furniture so you can decide where you would like it to go. Take a photo of this to use for reference.

4 Put the wallpaper to one side. Lay dust sheets over anything you don't want to get paint on and spray the furniture in the spray paint of your choice. Apply lightly and build up layers rather than spraying one thick layer of paint.

TIPS

Decoupage is traditionally fixed using a PVA solution (50 per cent glue, 50 per cent water) but when using wallpaper this can leave patches of transparency and ruin the finish. Here the wallpaper was fixed with extra strong wallpaper paste and then had a PVA wash over the top when it was in place.

Never attempt to trim pieces of wallpaper when it is wet, as it will rip. Wait until it is dry and cut with a craft knife.

For a matte finish, use a water-based emulsion paint and matte varnish.

5 Leave the paint to dry for 24 hours. Apply a thin layer of wallpaper paste over the furniture where you will be sticking the wallpaper and then, strip-by-strip, paste the wallpaper. Lightly paste each piece, place it in position on the piece of furniture and then using a paintbrush (or roller) smooth it out, getting rid of any air bubbles. This is harder than it sounds so make sure you do it thoroughly. Wipe off excess paste with a slightly damp sponge. At this stage make sure you make any holes for door handles etc. as they're really difficult to find once it is all dry. Lastly use a PVA solution to wash over everything and seal it.

6 Once you have decoupaged the whole piece and finished with a PVA wash, leave it to dry. Trim off any edges that are sticking out with a very sharp craft knife (this may happen as the wallpaper will probably have stretched when you pasted it). When all edges are neat and tidy, go over them again with the PVA solution to seal. Leave to dry.

7 The final step is to lacquer. Using a tough gloss varnish/lacquer, paint a layer of varnish over the entire piece of furniture, including any painted area, as this will protect the paint as well as the decoupaged areas. Repeat this between two and six times to create a hard layer, making the furniture super durable.

BOTANICAL BOXES

Make these exquisite floral storage boxes to keep jewellery, make-up and other odds and ends secure.

MATERIALS

- Plain cardboard boxes with lids
- Decorative paper
- Sharp scissors
- Acrylic paint and small paintbrush
- PVA (white) glue, diluted 50:50 with water
- Glue brush
- Varnish
- Kitchen paper
- Plastic sheet or newspaper

1 Protect your work surface with a plastic sheet or newspaper. Give the boxes a couple of coats of acrylic paint – you can use household paint, or artists' acrylics, but make sure you leave plenty of drying time between coats. Try not to let the paint layers get too thick, especially if the lids are a tight fit.

2 Select suitable images. Botanical illustrations were used in this project because they depicted several different stages of a plant's development, as well as cross-sections. These were used to create a boxed set with different pictures on each one that still worked together as a whole.

Make sure the images fit comfortably on the box lids and cut out carefully with small, sharp scissors – if there are isolated white areas cut them out first, before the image becomes too fragile.

3 Use a flat-ended and fairly stiff glue brush to 'stab' the glue onto the wrong side of the cutout images. This prevents the paper from stretching as it gets wet and will give a smoother finish.

4 Carefully position the images and smooth down to get rid of any wrinkles with your fingers. If there is any excess glue, wipe off with a piece of slightly damp kitchen paper.

5 When everything has had time to thoroughly dry, add a thin coat or two of varnish.

TIP
You could use spray varnish to speed up the finishing time.

RETRO CHAIR

In this quirky project, the decoupaged image was deliberately chosen to accentuate the chair's retro style.

MATERIALS

- A 1960s-style plywood chair (we used a copy of a classic Arne Jacobsen Series 7 chair)
- A poster big enough to cover the chair
- Multi-purpose spray paint or oil-based gloss paint
- Sandpaper (if necessary)
- Tracing paper and coloured crayon
- Reusable adhesive putty
- Pen or pencil
- PVA (white) glue, diluted 50:50 with water
- Paintbrush x 2
- Small roller
- Slightly damp sponge
- High-gloss varnish
- Dust sheet or newspaper
- Decorator's mask

TIPS

You don't need to use a roller but it is the most effective way to remove air bubbles. If you are very careful you can smooth out bubbles using a stiff, wet paintbrush and/or your hands (make sure they are wet so the paper doesn't tear).

It is advisable to wear a decorator's mask when spray painting.

1 Prepare the chair for painting by checking that the surfaces are scratch free, as spray paint will show up any scratches. Rub out any scratches lightly with fine-grade sandpaper if necessary. Then clean the chair so it is free of dirt and dust.

2 Lay down the dust sheet or newspaper and put the face mask on. Then, using light layers (follow the instructions on the can), build up the colour on the back, legs and any edges of the chair. Remember: the poster will cover the whole seat of the chair so it doesn't need to be painted. The finish is better with spray paint but you can paint the back and legs of the chair by hand using a tough oil-based gloss paint if you prefer. Leave to dry completely.

3 Now cover the seat of the chair with the sheet of tracing paper (this should be big enough to cover the seat of the chair) and stick it in place with reusable adhesive putty. Using a crayon, rub the chair edges so that when you remove the tracing paper the shape of the chair is left on the paper. Cut this shape out, then check that it fits the seat of the chair exactly as you don't want any mistakes later on.

4 Lay the tracing paper over the poster and draw around it with a pencil (you could stick it in place with reusable adhesive putty so it doesn't move). Make sure you pick a bit of the poster that will look good on the chair seat.

5 It is important to establish whether the chair's surface is completely flat (it probably won't be as the chair is likely to be shaped in some way). If it isn't, you will need to cut the poster into a jigsaw and apply each piece separately otherwise it won't stick properly. Try to cut along actual lines in the image (here we cut along the girl's legs, arms and edges of clothing), as lines cut on plain areas of the poster will be much more visible. Cut into approximately five or six pieces.

6 Apply a thin layer of diluted PVA over the whole seat of the chair, then spread a thin layer over the back of the first piece of poster you want to attach. Leave for five minutes before sticking to reduce the risk of the paper warping and bubbling. Carefully position the paper and, using wet hands or a clean, wet paintbrush, brush out any creases and bubbles (think of it like putting wallpaper up). Then, using the rubber roller, go over it in a few different directions to ensure all the bubbles are out. Do this with each piece of poster until it is all stuck to the chair. Wipe over very gently with a clean, slightly damp sponge to remove excess glue and leave to dry completely.

7 Finish by applying varnish. Paint one coat over the entire chair, back and legs included to give it added protection. Then apply another five to ten layers of varnish to the chair seat. This will ensure that it is completely sealed and make it hard-wearing enough to be used.

DRESSING SCREEN

Give an old-fashioned dressing screen an instant lift with beautiful paper and pastel paint to match.

MATERIALS

- Dressing screen
- Wallpaper scraps
- Eggshell paint
- Paintbrushes
- Scissors and craft knife
- PVA (white) glue, diluted 50:50 with water
- Varnish
- Slightly damp sponge
- Dust sheet or newspaper

1 Lay down the dust sheet and paint the back of the screen with eggshell paint (don't forget to do the sides, top and bottom as well). Leave to dry overnight.

2 Select between three and four different wallpapers to complement your paint. Cut into rectangles of similar size.

3 Once you have decided on the order you want the paper to be laid out, start gluing the pieces, making sure you cover right up to or even beyond each edge. Overlap them slightly to ensure none of the original screen can be seen. Paste more glue over the top of each piece of paper as you go – this will give the decoupage a nice finish. Wipe off excess glue with a slightly damp sponge. Leave to dry overnight.

4 Use a craft knife to carefully score around the edges of any overhanging paper and discard.

5 Using a clear varnish and paintbrush, cover the front of the screen. Leave to dry for at least 24 hours.

RING

This pretty patterned cat button makes a colourful ring. Any button with an interesting shape can be used for this project.

MATERIALS

- 1 x cat-shaped plastic button
- 1 x ring with ⅜in (9mm) flat pad
- Small piece of patterned paper
- 2in (50mm) square of sandpaper
- PVA (white) glue, diluted 50:50 with water
- Small paintbrush
- Container for glue
- Strong adhesive glue
- Small sharp scissors
- Pencil
- Craft knife
- Cutting mat
- Dust sheet or newspaper

TIP
Use this same technique to make ear studs by gluing the decoupage cat to a stud with a flat pad.

1 Lay out a dust sheet on your work surface to protect it. Sand the front of the button to provide a key for the decoupage.

2 With the patterned paper and a pencil, draw an outline of the cat button on the back of the paper. Take time to work out which part of the pattern you want on the cat.

3 Cut out the cat shape, leaving a margin of approximately ⅛in (3mm) around the outside of the pencil line. After cutting the shape out, go around the edge and make several small cuts up to the pencil line to form lots of little tabs. This helps the paper bend around the shape when it is glued on.

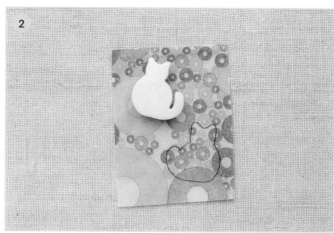

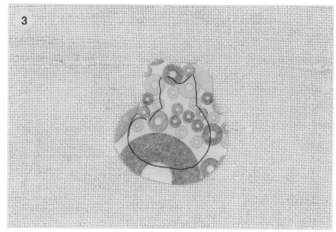

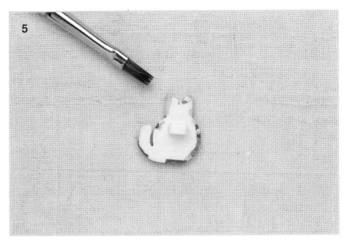

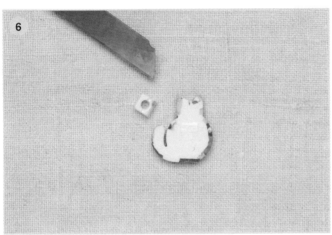

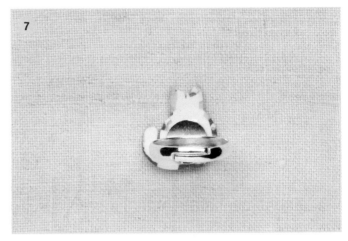

4 Pour a small amount of diluted PVA glue into a container and paint a layer of glue on the front of the cat button. Hold the button by the shank on the back and carefully place the paper on the cat, lining up the pencil outline to the edge of the cat. Paint a layer of glue over the top of the paper.

5 With a tiny amount of glue on the brush, go around the edge and paste each tab down the sides. Work slowly and make sure you take off any spare glue with the brush as you go.
to dry completely.

6 Take the craft knife and carefully cut the shank off the back of the button. As it's plastic it should be fairly easy to cut off.

7 Take the ring blank and sand the flat pad, then place a small amount of strong adhesive glue on the pad and stick the cat button down. Leave to dry completely before wearing.

TIPS
If the button is made of soft plastic, you can cut off the shank with an old pair of side cutters. Don't use a new pair of cutters as it could blunt them.

This design works with buttons that have holes, too; just follow the steps but skip step 6. The paper will cover the holes and the glue will fill them when attached to the ring blank.

BANGLE

This is the perfect project to revamp old bangles, but you can also buy blank bangles in wood or plastic in any size or style you like.

MATERIALS

- Bangle
- 3 x different sheets of standard size wrapping paper
- Ruler, pencil and scissors
- White (PVA) glue, diluted 50:50 with water
- Glue brush
- Clear varnish
- Dust sheet or newspaper

1 Cut out squares of about 1¼ x 1¼in (3 x 3cm), and smaller, of images from different wrapping papers. Also cut some thinner strips and rectangles, no longer than 2in (5cm), of other patterns from the wrapping paper to fill in the gaps between the images.

2 Lay out a dust sheet to protect your work surface. Take the first square of wrapping paper and brush a generous amount of glue all over the back of it.

3 Stick the paper onto the bangle. Apply a generous amount of glue to the brush and cover the front of the image, going over the edges onto the bangle.

4 Add another two pieces of wrapping paper to the bangle and stick down using the glue. Use your finger to smooth the paper down flat and push out any wrinkles. Make sure that all of the paper is stuck to the bangle.

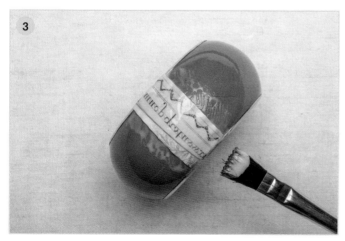

TIPS

When choosing the images for your bangle, stick to complementary colours, styles or themes to produce a seamless design.

Pour the glue into a pot and cover the surface you are working on as this can get messy!

5 Overlap the edges of the bangle with the images and fold them around so they stick to the inside. This makes a neat edge and continues the decoration so no gaps show through at all.

6 Keep adding images and glue as above, slightly overlapping them and with some of them diagonal, until every bit of the bangle is covered. Leave to dry fully.

7 Cut four strips from the same sheet of paper the width of the inside of the bangle and about 2¾in (7cm) in length.

8 Using the same technique as before, stick the strips of paper on the inside of the bangle to cover it completely. Smooth the strips down but don't worry if there are few wrinkles; it is less important on the inside. Leave to dry.

9 Finish with a coat of clear varnish to seal the paper.

BROOCH

Domino tiles make fantastic bases for small decoupage and are the perfect shape for making brooches. The possibilities are endless.

MATERIALS
- Domino and patterned paper
- Pencil and small, sharp scissors
- PVA (white) glue, diluted 50:50 with water
- Small paintbrush
- Craft stick or popsicle stick
- Varnish
- 1in (25mm) pin back
- Superglue
- Dust sheet or newspaper

TIP
Wooden domino tiles make the best base but are quite hard to find. Try thrift stores or Internet auction sites.

1 Lay out a dust sheet or newspaper to protect your work surface. Place the domino onto the paper and trace around the edges. Use small scissors to cut the paper to shape.

2 Smear PVA glue onto the domino using a small paintbrush.

3 Top the domino with the piece of paper and smooth down with your finger.

4 Apply more glue to the paper and smear over the surface using a wooden craft stick or popsicle stick.

5 When the paper is dry, apply a layer of high-gloss varnish onto the surface of the paper using a stick or a small paintbrush. Leave to dry completely.

6 Finally, use superglue to stick the pin back to the back of the domino.

TECHNIQUES

Decoupage has long graced the pages of craft magazines and craft tutorials alike. You can decoupage almost anything, from bangles to boxes and big items of furniture, so long as glue will stick to it. If you choose your papers carefully, you will end up with a stylish piece that looks hand crafted.

There are two ways of decorating using decoupage – to completely cover the object in images, which is the more usual method, or to pick out one or two images to add interest to something plain. If you plan to use the second method, the decoupage will look much better if you choose something like a flower to cut out and stick on, rather than a square-edged picture.

WHAT TO USE

Just about any materials can be used for decoupage, including newspaper, sheet music, comics, cards, old maps, tissue paper, wrapping paper, wallpaper, paper shopping bags, magazines, fabric… even junk mail, flyers, seed packets, old food labels or sweet wrappers! You can also buy special decoupage paper, which is thin like tissue paper but has the strength of standard paper and does not tear when wet with glue.

Don't use anything that's been printed on an ink-jet printer as the colour will run when glued. Also, make sure that thin papers are only printed on one side, or the pattern on the reverse may show through once glued.

Generally, the softer and more flexible the material, the easier it'll be to work with, particularly if you're covering a curved surface. You want to keep the surface as smooth as possible so it's best to avoid using anything too thick. If you need to cover a large surface very quickly, use wallpaper or rolls of thin fabric. These can also be used as a background before adding other decoupaged items on top.

You can use whole pieces of paper, you can tear it, or you can cut the paper to make interesting shapes and designs.

How to tear paper
Tearing the paper will help to create smoother edges. Fold the paper along the tear-line and create a strong crease with your fingernail. Repeat in the opposite direction, and then tear the paper.

How to cut paper
Use scissors or a craft knife to cut around out the shapes, holding the scissors so that they are angled slightly to the right. This will create a smoother, bevelled edge.

GLUES AND VARNISHES

Once upon a time, decoupage entailed the use of toxic glues and fragile shellacs that would yellow with age; thankfully today's makers have the benefit of cheap and easy water-based PVA (white) glue that can also double as a varnish. Decoupage glue is an all-in-one glue, sealer and gloss finish. However, this is quite expensive so a solution of PVA glue diluted 50:50 with water is fine to use instead. Just mix up some PVA glue and water in a small bowl or add to a clean glass jar, put the lid on and shake to mix. You can finish your work with a PVA solution too to make it hard-wearing, but be aware that this won't be waterproof so you may prefer to use a varnish instead.

TIP
Glue takes much longer to dry than you think. It will touch dry within a matter of minutes but it needs to be completely dry before you apply further coats of glue. Items of furniture that have been decoupaged need to be left for at least 24 hours before using.

BRUSHES

A hog's hair flat-edged brush or similar is perfect for gluing but you can use any brush you like, so long as it is appropriate for the size of the pieces you are gluing. A small artist's paintbrush is ideal for delicate cutouts, such as in the chest of drawers project (see page 14), whereas for a project like the wine box (see page 10) it's better to use a more robust general-purpose paintbrush.

The most important thing to remember is to never let glue dry on the brush you use, because it will ruin it. If you rinse the brush thoroughly in water you will be able to reuse it for other projects.

PLANNING THE DECOUPAGE

Don't feel you have to cover the surface area with cutouts – you could use just a few for special effects (see Antiqued Shelves, page 17 and Botanical Boxes, page 28). In this case, plan the project by making a preliminary sketch of the layout or put the cutouts into place without gluing them and take a photo to remember the arrangement. Also, consider the colour and texture of the things you are gluing.

PREPARATION

Make sure the object you want to decoupage is clean and completely dry before you start. Cover your work surface with suitable protection. Fill in deep gouges, and sand it down to remove bumps and imperfections if necessary. A primer coat of latex paint will help cutouts stick better to materials such as metal or wood.

MISCELLANEOUS

You'll also need a pair of scissors, a craft knife with a sharp blade, a tape measure or ruler, pencil, sandpaper, and something to protect your work surface, such as a dust sheet, plastic sheeting or old newspaper. For delicate cutouts, a cutting mat and a scalpel is a must. A slightly damp sponge, cloth or kitchen paper to mop up excess glue is essential, too.

HOW TO DO DECOUPAGE

1 Apply the glue. Use a paintbrush or glue brush to brush a thin layer of PVA glue, diluted 50:50 with water, onto the surface and onto the backs of the cutouts. Make sure you apply the glue evenly and over the edges of the cutouts. If you 'stab' the glue, it prevents the paper from stretching as it gets wet and will give a smoother finish. To minimize warping and bubbling, it helps to leave the paper for a few minutes before applying to the item you want to cover.

2 Glue the cutouts, piece-by-piece, to the object. Lay a piece of your cut paper onto the area to which you applied the glue. Apply the paper carefully to avoid bending or crumpling it, and smooth it out with a brayer (a small roller) or with a craft or popsicle stick, rubbing outward from the centre. You don't have to use a rubber roller but it is the most effective way to remove air bubbles. You could also smooth out bubbles using a stiff, wet paintbrush or your fingers/hands (make sure they are wet so the paper doesn't tear). Repeat with each piece. Keep a damp cloth or sponge handy

to wipe off spilled or excess glue and to help press down the edges of cutouts when you glue them down.

3 Let the glue dry. If you are applying several layers, make sure each layer is completely dry before starting on the next.

4 Once the glue is dry, rub your hand over the surface, feeling for peeled up corners, wrinkles, or papers that may feel as if they are not sticking. If there is a rim or an edge that the decoupage wraps around, you can trim it with a razor for a cleaner look. If you're having trouble making the cutouts stick, brush a thin layer of diluted PVA glue over the entire surface.

5 Seal the decoupage with an appropriate sealant, such as specially formulated decoupage finish (available at art and craft stores) or varnish. You can use diluted PVA but although it will be hard-wearing, it won't be waterproof. Let each coat dry thoroughly before applying the next, and leave for 24 hours after the final coat before using.